Publications directors : Isabelle Jeuge-Maynart and Ghislaine Stora
Editorial director : Émilie Franc
Editor : Alice Dauphin
Graphic design and cover : Aurore Elie
Typesetting : Lucile Jouret
Production : Donia Faiz

**The abuse of alcohol is dangerous for health;
consume with moderation.**

40 Cocktails Selected by

COCKTAIL BOOK

The Shelby Company Ltd

40 Cocktails Selected by

COCKTAIL BOOK

The Shelby Company Ltd

Sandrine Houdré-Grégoire
Photography by Charly Deslandes

WHITE LION PUBLISHING

CONTENTS

Whiskey

Gin

Other spirits

Whiskey

VENDETTA

FOR 1 GLASS – PREPARATION: 5 MINUTES

40 ml (1⅓ fl oz) whisky

20 ml (⅔ fl oz) amaretto

20 ml (⅔ fl oz) maraschino liqueur

1 brandied cherry, for garnish (optional)

Pour the whisky and the liqueurs into a mixing glass filled with ice. Stir with a bar spoon and pour into a cocktail glass.

If desired, garnish with a brandied cherry.

RED HORSE

FOR 1 GLASS – PREPARATION: 5 MINUTES

30 ml (1 fl oz) fresh orange juice
30 ml (1 fl oz) red Italian vermouth
(such as Martini or Cinzano)
30 ml (1 fl oz) Cherry Heering Liqueur
30 ml (1 fl oz) Sexton Single Malt Irish Whiskey

Into a shaker filled with ice, pour
the orange juice, vermouth,
liqueur and the whiskey.

Shake and pour through a
strainer into a cocktail glass
without ice.

JOHN SHELBY

FOR 1 GLASS – PREPARATION: 5 MINUTES

20 ml (⅔ fl oz) green Chartreuse
20 ml (⅔ fl oz) Applejack
60 ml (2 fl oz) rye whiskey
1 slice of dried apple

Into a mixing glass filled with ice, pour the
Chartreuse, Applejack and the rye whiskey.
Mix with a bar spoon.

2

Pour into a cocktail glass along
with a slice of dried apple.

BIRMINGHAM SOUR

FOR 1 GLASS – PREPARATION: 5 MINUTES

30 ml (1 fl oz) lemon juice, freshly squeezed

20 ml (⅔ fl oz) cane sugar syrup

10 ml (⅓ fl oz) red wine

60 ml (2 fl oz) rye whiskey

Into a shaker filled with ice, pour the lemon juice, sugar syrup, red wine and rye whiskey.

Shake, then pour through a strainer into an old fashioned glass.

ADA SHELBY

FOR 1 GLASS – PREPARATION: 5 MINUTES

40 ml (1⅓ fl oz) Sexton Single Malt Irish Whiskey

15 ml (½ fl oz) triple sec (such as Cointreau)

15 ml (½ fl oz) strawberry liqueur

20 ml (⅔ fl oz) fresh orange juice

 Into a shaker filled with ice, pour the whiskey, the liqueurs and the orange juice.

 Shake and pour through a strainer into a wine or cocktail glass.

THE SHELBY JULEP

FOR 1 GLASS – PREPARATION: 5 MINUTES

15 fresh mint leaves, plus 1 sprig for garnish

1 teaspoon brown sugar

60 ml (2 fl oz) rye whiskey

30 ml (1 fl oz) peach brandy

Place the mint leaves and the brown sugar directly into a julep cup and crush. Fill with crushed ice, then pour over the rye whiskey and the peach brandy.

Stir with a bar spoon and garnish with a fresh sprig of mint.

EASY DIZZY

FOR 1 GLASS — PREPARATION: 10 MINUTES

80 ml (2⅔ fl oz) Earl Grey tea

1 teaspoon orange marmalade

10 ml (⅓ fl oz) Bénédictine

40 ml (1⅓ fl oz) Irish whiskey

1

Boil some water, leave it
to cool for a moment, then
make a cup of Earl Grey tea.

2

Put the marmalade directly into a
glass. Pour over the liqueur and
the whiskey, followed by the tea
while still hot. Stir and enjoy.

MR SABINI

FOR 1 GLASS – PREPARATION: 5 MINUTES

40 ml (1⅓ fl oz) rye whiskey

30 ml (1 fl oz) Campari

30 ml (1 fl oz) red Italian vermouth

(such as Martini or Cinzano)

Orange twist, for garnish

Into a mixing glass filled with ice, pour the rye whiskey, Campari and red vermouth.

Mix using a bar spoon and strain into a sherry cobbler glass with ice. Garnish with the orange twist.

THE 1919

FOR 1 GLASS – PREPARATION: 5 MINUTES

40 ml (1⅓ fl oz) Sexton Single Malt Irish Whiskey

20 ml (⅔ fl oz) Noilly Prat

20 ml (⅔ fl oz) green crème de menthe

20 ml (⅔ fl oz) green Chartreuse

Into a shaker filled with ice, pour the whiskey, the Noilly Prat, the crème de menthe and the Chartreuse.

Shake well and pour through a strainer into a Champagne coupe or saucer, or a cocktail glass.

SECTION D

FOR 1 GLASS – PREPARATION: 5 MINUTES

2 dashes of Angostura Aromatic Bitters

30 ml (1 fl oz) red Italian vermouth

(such as Martini or Cinzano)

50 ml (2½ fl oz) maraschino liqueur

60 ml (2 fl oz) Sexton Single Malt Irish Whiskey

1 brandied cherry, for garnish (optional)

1

Into a mixing glass filled with ice, pour the bitters, the vermouth, the maraschino liqueur and the whiskey.

2

Mix using a bar spoon and pour through a strainer into a wine or cocktail glass. If desired, garnish with a brandied cherry.

INSPECTOR CAMPBELL

FOR 1 GLASS – PREPARATION: 5 MINUTES

10 ml (⅓ fl oz) absinthe

2 dashes of Peychaud's Aromatic Bitters

2 dashes of Angostura Aromatic Bitters

20 ml (⅔ fl oz) red Italian vermouth
(such as Martini or Cinzano)

30 ml (1 fl oz) Bénédictine

40 ml (1⅓ fl oz) rye whiskey

Put the absinthe into a small spray bottle. Pour the bitters, vermouth, Bénédictine and rye whiskey into a mixing glass filled with ice.

Mix using a bar spoon and strain into a cocktail glass. Finish it off with a spray of absinthe over the liquid in the glass.

FREDDIE THORNE

FOR 1 GLASS – PREPARATION: 5 MINUTES

15 fresh mint leaves, plus 1 sprig for garnish
30 ml (1 fl oz) cane sugar syrup
Juice of ½ a lime
60 ml (2 fl oz) Sexton Single Malt Irish Whiskey
10 ml (⅓ fl oz) Fernet-Branca

1

Into a tall glass, place the mint leaves, sugar syrup and lime juice. Crush them together using a pestle.

2

Fill the glass with crushed ice, pour in the whiskey and stir using a bar spoon. Finish with the Fernet-Branca and garnish with an extra sprig of mint.

ULSTER FORCE

FOR 1 GLASS – PREPARATION: 5 MINUTES

2 sprigs of fresh thyme
15 ml (½ fl oz) honey syrup
40 ml (1⅓ fl oz) apple juice
40 ml (1⅓ fl oz) malt whiskey
1 dash of Angostura Aromatic Bitters

Light one of the thyme sprigs using a
match or lighter, and place it in a shaker.

Pour in the syrup, apple juice, whiskey
and bitters, and shake for about ten
seconds. Pour through a strainer into a
cocktail glass or tall wine glass. Light
the second sprig of thyme and serve
on the glass.

BILLY KIMBER

FOR 1 GLASS – PREPARATION: 5 MINUTES

30 ml (1 fl oz) Bushmills Black Bush
20 ml (⅔ fl oz) triple sec (such as Cointreau)
Malt beer
Ground cinnamon

1
Into a beer glass filled with ice, pour the
Bushmills Black Bush and the triple sec.

2
Finish off with the malt beer and dust
with ground cinnamon.

DANNY WHIZZ-BANG

FOR 1 GLASS – PREPARATION: 5 MINUTES

10 ml (⅓ fl oz) Monin Pink
Peppercorn Syrup
20 ml (⅔ fl oz) grapefruit juice
20 ml (⅔ fl oz) dry Cinzano
40 ml (1⅓ fl oz) rye whiskey

1

Into a shaker half-filled with ice, pour the
syrup, the grapefruit juice, the dry Cinzano
and the whiskey.

2

Shake and pour through a strainer
into a cocktail or wine glass.

Gin

LAST WORLD

FOR 1 GLASS – PREPARATION: 5 MINUTES

10 ml (⅓ fl oz) fresh lime juice
30 ml (1 fl oz) green Chartreuse
30 ml (1 fl oz) gin
20 ml (⅔ fl oz) maraschino liqueur

1

Into a shaker filled with ice, pour the lime juice, Chartreuse, gin and maraschino liqueur.

2

Shake and strain into a cocktail or wine glass.

E P S O M

FOR 1 GLASS – PREPARATION: 5 MINUTES

1 egg white
40 ml (1⅓ fl oz) gin
20 ml (⅔ fl oz) Giffard Parfait Amour Liqueur
20 ml (⅔ fl oz) Cherry Marnier Liqueur
10 ml (⅓ fl oz) lemon juice,
freshly squeezed
Tonic water

Place the egg white into a shaker
with no ice and shake. Add some ice
cubes, along with the gin, the liqueurs
and the lemon juice.

Shake and pour through a strainer
into a stemmed beer glass with no
ice. Top up with the tonic water.

CHANGRETTA

FOR 1 GLASS – PREPARATION: 5 MINUTES

60 ml (2 fl oz) London Dry Gin

60 ml (2 fl oz) red Italian vermouth

(such as Martini or Cinzano)

2 dashes of Fernet-Branca

1 slice of fresh orange, for garnish

1

Into a mixing glass filled with ice cubes,
pour the gin, vermouth and Fernet-Branca.
Mix well using a bar spoon.

2

Pour into a Champagne coupe or saucer,
garnishing with a slice of orange.

THE GARRISON

FOR 1 GLASS – PREPARATION: 5 MINUTES

40 ml (1⅓ fl oz) gin

15 ml (½ fl oz) cane sugar syrup

15 ml (½ fl oz) lemon juice,
freshly squeezed

20 ml (⅔ fl oz) blackberry liqueur

1 fresh blackberry, for garnish

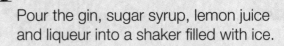

1

Pour the gin, sugar syrup, lemon juice
and liqueur into a shaker filled with ice.

2

Mix well and pour through a
strainer into a cocktail glass.
Garnish with a blackberry.

CHARLES STRONG

FOR 1 GLASS – PREPARATION: 5 MINUTES

60 ml (2 fl oz) London Dry Gin
10 ml (⅓ fl oz) dry vermouth
1 cocktail onion

1

Into a mixing glass filled with ice cubes,
pour the gin and the vermouth.
Mix using a bar spoon.

2

Strain into a cocktail glass, and then
drop the cocktail onion into the glass.

BONNIE GOLD

FOR 1 GLASS – PREPARATION: 5 MINUTES

40 ml (1⅓ fl oz) London Dry Gin

20 ml (⅔ fl oz) Giffard Menthe-Pastille Liqueur

15 ml (½ fl oz) fresh lime juice

60 ml (2 fl oz) tonic water

1 dash of Peychaud's Aromatic Bitters

1 sprig of fresh mint, for garnish

Into a tall, ice-filled glass, pour the gin,
the liqueur, the lime juice, the tonic water
and the bitters.

Stir together with a bar spoon and
garnish with a sprig of mint.

TOMMY SHELBY

FOR 1 GLASS – PREPARATION: 5 MINUTES

3 dashes of orange bitters

60 ml (2 fl oz) Noilly Prat

40 ml (1⅓ fl oz) Old Tom Gin

Lemon twist

Into a mixing glass, pour the orange bitters, Noilly Prat and gin. Mix well.

Pour into a tumbler glass filled with ice, then squeeze the lemon twist over the glass and drop it in.

ARTHUR'S COFFEE

FOR 1 GLASS – PREPARATION: 5 MINUTES

3 cardamom pods
20 ml (⅔ fl oz) coffee liqueur
50 ml (2½ fl oz) gin
50 ml (2½ fl oz) cold espresso coffee
Coffee beans, for garnish

Crush the cardamom pods and place
them with coffee liqueur into a shaker.
Fill the shaker with ice, then pour in the
gin and the coffee.

Shake and pour into a cocktail glass.
Garnish with coffee beans.

MICHAEL GRAY

FOR 1 GLASS – PREPARATION: 5 MINUTES

1 egg white

40 ml (1⅓ fl oz) gin

20 ml (⅔ fl oz) triple sec (such as Cointreau)

20 ml (⅔ fl oz) white crème de cacao

Zest of 1 lemon

Place the egg white into a shaker with no ice and shake. Add ice cubes, along with the gin, the liqueurs and the lemon zest.

Shake and pour through a strainer into a cocktail glass.

MRS ROSS

30 ml (1 fl oz) green tea
40 ml (1⅓ fl oz) cucumber-infused gin (see note)
20 ml (⅔ fl oz) ginger liqueur
30 ml (1 fl oz) pear nectar

Make an infusion of green tea
and leave to cool.

2

Into a shaker filled with ice, pour the gin,
the liqueur, the green tea and the pear
nectar. Shake and pour through a strainer
into a cocktail glass.

Note
Place 3 thick slices of cucumber
into a bottle of gin. Leave to infuse for
24 hours then strain.

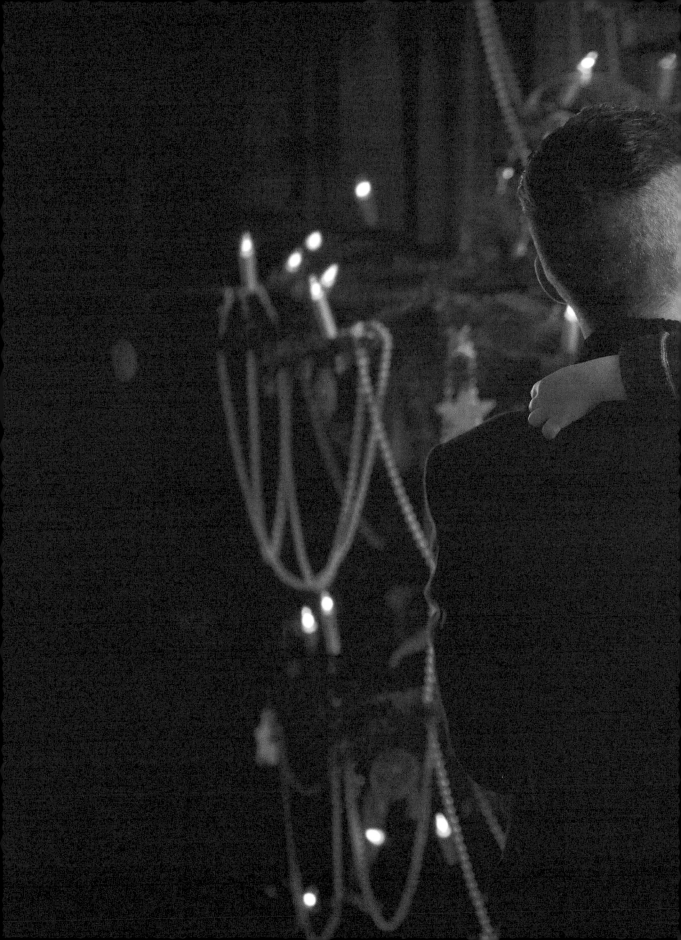

GRACE'S SECRET

FOR 1 GLASS – PREPARATION: 5 MINUTES

60 ml (2 fl oz) London Dry Gin
30 ml (1 fl oz) red Italian vermouth
(such as Martini or Cinzano)
10 ml (⅓ fl oz) elderflower liqueur
2 dashes of peach bitters
Lemon twist, for garnish

1

Into a mixing glass filled with ice, pour the gin, vermouth, elderflower liqueur and bitters. Mix together using a bar spoon.

2

Pour through a strainer into a cocktail glass without ice. Squeeze the lemon twist into the glass before using it for garnish.

SCRAP

FOR 1 GLASS – PREPARATION: 5 MINUTES

6 juniper berries
20 ml (⅔ fl oz) lemon juice, freshly squeezed
40 ml (1⅓ fl oz) gin
20 ml (⅔ fl oz) Byrrh (red vermouth)
10 ml (⅓ fl oz) cane sugar syrup
2 dashes of celery bitters
2 dashes of lemon bitters
Tonic water
1 slice of cucumber, for garnish

Place the juniper berries and lemon juice directly into an old-fashioned glass and crush gently. Pour in the gin, Byrrh, sugar syrup and the bitters.

Mix together using a bar spoon. Add ice cubes and top up with the tonic water. Garnish with a slice of cucumber.

BLACK COUNTRY

FOR 1 GLASS — PREPARATION: 5 MINUTES — INFUSION: 24 HOURS

15 ml (½ fl oz) cane sugar syrup
30 ml (1 fl oz) lemon juice, freshly squeezed
30 ml (1 fl oz) wild strawberry liqueur
50 ml (2½ fl oz) black pepper-infused gin (see note)
1 fresh strawberry, for garnish (optional)

1

Into a shaker filled with ice, pour the
sugar syrup, the freshly squeezed lemon
juice, the strawberry liqueur and the gin.

2

Shake and pour into a glass.
If desired, garnish with a strawberry.

Note   Place 25 black peppercorns
into a bottle of gin. Leave to infuse
for 24 hours, then strain.

REVOLUTION

FOR 1 GLASS – PREPARATION: 5 MINUTES

30 ml (1 fl oz) Lillet Blanc
30 ml (1 fl oz) triple sec (such as Cointreau)
40 ml (1⅓ fl oz) London Dry Gin
30 ml (1 fl oz) lemon juice, freshly squeezed
1 dash of absinthe

Into a shaker filled with ice cubes pour all of the ingredients except the absinthe. Shake.

Swirl the dash of absinthe around a stemmed beer glass or an old-fashioned glass, then strain the contents of the shaker into the glass and add some ice.

FIVE BELLS

FOR 1 GLASS – PREPARATION: 5 MINUTES

30 ml (1 fl oz) London Dry Gin

30 ml (1 fl oz) green Chartreuse

30 ml (1 fl oz) red Italian vermouth

(such as Martini or Cinzano)

3 dashes of orange bitters

Lemon twist, for garnish

Into a mixing glass filled with ice, pour the gin, Chartreuse, vermouth and bitters. Stir together using a bar spoon.

Pour through a strainer into a sherry cobbler glass with no ice. Garnish and flavour by squeezing the lemon twist over the top of the glass.

Other
spirits

WEST HIGH

FOR 1 GLASS – PREPARATION: 5 MINUTES

60 ml (2 fl oz) smoked tea (such as
Lapsang souchong), cold
1 teaspoon pine and fir tree honey
60 ml (2 fl oz) rum
Pine needles, for burning (optional)

The night before, brew a cup of smoked
tea and leave it to chill.

Into an old-fashioned glass containing
a large chunk of ice, pour the honey,
the tea and the rum. Mix together and
then burn the pine needles over the
top of the glass, if desired.

ANGEL

FOR 1 GLASS – PREPARATION: 5 MINUTES

50 ml (2½ fl oz) rum

10 ml (⅓ fl oz) rose syrup

Tonic water

1 dried rosebud, for garnish

Into a tall glass filled with ice cubes,
pour the rum and the rose syrup,
then top up with tonic water.

Stir together using a bar spoon,
and garnish with the dried rosebud.

DERBY

FOR 1 GLASS — PREPARATION: 5 MINUTES

60 ml (2 fl oz) Cognac
15 ml (½ fl oz) triple sec (such as Cointreau)
10 ml (⅓ fl oz) lemon juice, freshly squeezed,
plus zest for garnish
2 dashes of Angostura Aromatic Bitters
Sugar, for decoration

1

Into a shaker filled with ice, pour the
Cognac, the liqueur, the lemon juice
and the bitters. Shake.

2

Create a sugar frosted rim on a tall
stemmed glass and fill with crushed ice.
Strain the cocktail into the glass and
add slices of lemon zest.

GRAND DUKE

FOR 1 GLASS – PREPARATION: 5 MINUTES

20 ml (⅔ fl oz) Cognac

20 ml (⅔ fl oz) blackberry liqueur

10 ml (⅓ fl oz) lemon juice, freshly

squeezed, plus a slice of lemon, for garnish

60 ml (2 fl oz) red Burgundy wine

1 fresh blackberry, for garnish (optional)

Into an old-fashioned glass, place some ice cubes, along with the Cognac, blackberry liqueur, freshly squeezed lemon juice and finally the red wine.

Mix together using a bar spoon and garnish with the slice of lemon, and a blackberry if desired.

PIMM'S NUMBER 1

FOR 1 GLASS – PREPARATION: 10 MINUTES

1 slice of orange

1 slice of lemon

6 fresh mint leaves, plus 1 sprig for garnish

60 ml (2 fl oz) Pimm's No. 1 Cup

60 ml (2 fl oz) ginger ale

1 long sliver of cucumber, for garnish

Into a mixing glass, place the citrus fruits and the mint leaves, then pour in the Pimm's. Let rest for around ten minutes, then strain into a Pimm's cup filled with crushed ice.

Top up with the ginger ale, then add the lemon and orange slices and garnish with the cucumber and the mint sprig.

BY ORDER OF
THE PEAKY BLINDERS

FOR 1 GLASS – PREPARATION: 10 MINUTES

80 ml (2⅔ fl oz) pink grapefruit juice,
freshly squeezed
Salt
40 ml (1⅓ fl oz) amber rum
20 ml (⅔ fl oz) Galliano

Insert the rim of a tall glass into the
grapefruit used to make the juice,
then roll the glass in salt to create a
salt-frosted rim.

Fill the glass with ice cubes, add
the rum and the grapefruit juice
and finish off with the Galliano.

CHAMPAGNE COCKTAIL

FOR 1 GLASS – PREPARATION: 5 MINUTES

¼ sugar cube

3 dashes of Angostura Aromatic Bitters

40 ml (1⅓ fl oz) Cognac

120 ml (4⅓ fl oz) Champagne

Zest of 1 orange

Place the sugar cube at the bottom of a Champagne flute and soak in bitters. Pour in the Cognac and top up with Champagne.

Squeeze the orange zest over and drop it into the glass.

TATIANA

FOR 1 GLASS – PREPARATION: 5 MINUTES

40 ml (1⅓ fl oz) vodka, chilled

10 ml (⅓ fl oz) Giffard Parfait Amour Liqueur

80 ml (2⅔ fl oz) Champagne, chilled

1 fresh strawberry, for garnish

1

Directly into a Champagne flute, pour the chilled vodka and the liqueur, then top up with the Champagne.

2

Serve with a strawberry for garnish.

SPARKLING SUZIE

FOR 1 GLASS – PREPARATION: 5 MINUTES

60 ml (2 fl oz) Suze Gentiane
1 slice of lemon, for garnish
120 ml (4⅓ fl oz) tonic water

Pour the Suze directly into a tall glass
filled with ice cubes.

Add the slice of lemon and top
up with tonic water.

GRACE SHELBY

FOR 1 GLASS – PREPARATION: 5 MINUTES

10 ml (⅓ fl oz) mango syrup
10 ml (⅓ fl oz) lemon juice,
freshly squeezed
20 ml (⅔ fl oz) yellow Chartreuse
40 ml (1⅓ fl oz) brandy

1

Into a shaker half-filled with ice cubes,
pour the mango syrup, the lemon juice,
the Chartreuse and the brandy.

2

Shake and pour through a strainer
into a cocktail glass with no ice.

INDEX

Brimming with creative inspiration, how-to projects and useful information to enrich your everyday life, Quarto Knows is a favourite destination for those pursuing their interests and passions. Visit our site and dig deeper with our books into your area of interest: Quarto Creates, Quarto Cooks, Quarto Homes, Quarto Lives, Quarto Drives, Quarto Explores, Quarto Gifts, or Quarto Kids.

First published in 2020 by White Lion Publishing,
an imprint of The Quarto Group.
The Old Brewery, 6 Blundell Street
London, N7 9BH,
United Kingdom
T (0)20 7700 6700
www.QuartoKnows.com

Original edition first published in French by Larousse in 2019
© Larousse 2019.
Translation © The Quarto Group 2020

Sandrine Houdré-Grégoire has asserted her moral right to be identified as the Author of this Work, in accordance with the Copyright, Designs and Patents Act 1988.

A catalogue record for this book is available from the British Library.

ISBN 978-0-7112-5871-6

10 9 8 7 6 5